MANI

111 Keys to Unlocking Your Divinity

BY

BRIAN HYPPOLITE

DEDICATIONS

To my brother Jelani, my children Samara and Leilani, Pap, and Chantel,

If I'm ever not here to guide you, come back and meet me here.

Together, we will get you where you need to be.

You are my legacy.

TABLE OF CONTENTS

PREFACE

"Bad seeds don't lead to good fruit/
You can't deny the proof when there's poison at the
root/
Some trees you just can't cut down; you gotta
uproot/
Truth sounds like hate to those who hate to hear the
truth."

To build independent, self-sustaining, African communities, we must first build, cultivate, and empower self-sustaining African individuals. The foundations on which our present day infrastructures have been erected not only divided us as a people but even divided us within our own selves. This detrimental disconnect from our divinity has had paralyzing effects.

Most of us have unknowingly resided in a state of completely false self-identification. Generations have perished from a lack of knowledge. More specifically, from a lack of knowledge of self. A knowledge of self creates a love of self. That love for self demands a respect of self. That respect of self will protect and cultivate the best environment

1

for self. But everything has a starting point, and in the marathon of self-mastery, a knowledge of self is the starting line.

As a society, our destruction has played out as we have played into the hands of unfruitful habits, characteristics, and desires we've come to value more than disturbing our present realities with awakening truths. If it only takes a lie three generations to outlive anyone who knows its falsehood, it's not at all hard to come to terms with the presence of fraudulent pretenses that we have been force - fed and have been formed within. Complete lies have become protected truths. What is known to be fake is now openly celebrated and rewarded, while originality and free thinking remains shunned in social settings. THIS ISN'T ALL YOUR FAULT! Much of the bad fruit hanging in the orchards of our lives were harvested from the seeds sown into our roots hundreds of years ago. If you are reading this, it is YOU who has been sent to uproot these prevarications and eradicate your family tree of the diseases running through its branches.

Once, on a mission's trip in my homeland, Haiti, I came across a goat with a yoke around its neck. The goat stood with a tiresome grimace at the opening of a four-foot, chain-link fence. I stopped my dirt bike and watched as the goat would back up and attempt to run through the gateway to freedom. The yoke, however, stretched farther than the width of the entryway, so neither ambition nor brute strength was enough to get him through. After shaking off the rattle of each failed effort, the goat would stare at the open dirt road, seemingly inches away, and convince itself to try again, only to feel the disappointment of another defeat. The yoke was doing exactly what it was created to do: restrict and burden.

I found myself at a parallel. I identified with the goat. I'd worn that tired face myself. I'd seen that same despair in the eyes of my people in Haiti as well as in the U.S. The yokes we wear are often made of generational curses and fastened by systematic slavery. Try as we might, many of us can't walk through the doors we need to and enter the space of freedom we should be in because we are wearing contraptions of bondage. That old beaten up yoke around the goat's neck undoubtedly preceded its hostage. In the same way, the limitations, trickery, and devices crafted to bind us were planned for us so long ago, the shackles are now on our minds and chains are no longer needed on our bodies.

Let's consider many of the behaviors, traits, habits, and characteristics we call our personality. They are actually learned behaviors we were either handed down or created in order to adapt to a toxic environment and/or traumatic situations/circumstances. More often than not, even as we emerge from and escape these sources of suffering, we take with us the mentalities and coping mechanisms we took on. Even an acute understanding of this summons up the question "Who, what, and how would you be if you existed outside the identity your trauma gave you?"

We were birthed into a gumbo of poverty, miseducation, psychological warfare, biological warfare, social/economic oppression, spiritual slavery, and broken homes within a broken nation littered with broken systems. Banish the expectation put on you to be "whole" when all you've been given is pieces to build yourself with. You will be whole, with nothing missing and nothing broken, but it will take some time like putting together all the pieces of the puzzle. Give yourself a little slack and a lot of love and admiration. Appreciate your growth as it is happening. I know it's uncomfortable, but its destiny and your divinity that is waiting on you to recognize and utilize it.

There's unmatched beauty and wisdom waiting in the acceptance of your flaws. Embrace your imperfections and learn from them. Growing pains come in all forms, but it is now your time and season of growth. We will dig deep, and as we journey inward, don't you dare overlook all the blessings you're surrounded by right now! You've come so far, and before we go any further, I want to tell you I'm so proud of you.

I wrote this book to help remove the yoke around your neck and release you into freedom: freedom of your heart, mind, and soul; freedom of your abilities; freedom to exist in your true identity; freedom to manifest YOU!

Throughout history, philosophers, scholars, master thinkers, teachers, creators, great minds and achievers have all unanimously agreed on one thing: Man is the master of his own universe because he is the master of his mind. Therefore, once he masters his mind, he can create any desired universe.

It is your time to unlock doors to success, wealth, happiness, peace, and legacy! The sacred keys to self-mastery await you within this soul-satisfying manual of inner work and elevation. Arm yourself with ancient understandings, timeless life lessons, and habits proven to be powerful for all who yield them.

This ancient understanding has become so far extinct that it is considered to be a novelty today. USE THIS TO YOUR ADVANTAGE! This book is a guide to your god state, superpower, divine nature, and purpose. Start your journey today and *Manifest You*!

CHAPTER ONE

MANIFESTING TOOLS
AND CHEAT CODES

Consider these first 11 keys to be prerequisites for your freedom and elevation. You are not responsible for the programming you received as a child, but you're 100% responsible for *fixing it* as an adult. If you aren't ready to do all of these right now, you probably won't see the results you desire. Let me tell you with love and compassion: If you don't like what you've been reaping, you'll have to change what you've been sowing.

KEY NUMBER ONE

Commit to your journey of self-development and alignment. You are your first line of defense! In a solid act of self-interest and preservation, you must be willing to abandon anything (or anyone) that is counterproductive to the reality you want. Love yourself with purpose and legacy so selfishly that you'd kill anything that threatens your future on sight—even the present-day version of yourself! You can't heal in the same environment you got sick in. That applies across physical, mental, and spiritual realms.

KEY NUMBER TWO

Give yourself some space. Commit to alone time! You will need to recharge, reevaluate, and reposition your heart and mind several times throughout this course. This will require reserving a daily portion of your time to your evolution. The less outside influences the better. Cut back on the radio, the phone, the tv, and even the friends and extended family. You need time and space to grow in this season freely without the opinions and frequencies of others.

KEY NUMBER THREE

Prepare your mind and emotions to confront and release hurt, resentment, and regrets in order to clear mental blockages. Holistic healing involves touching parts of yourself that terrify you. Real growth occurs when you start checking yourself instead of blaming others. You take your power back by being utterly responsible for your life.

KEY NUMBER FOUR

Establish new and healthy connections that support your new vision and reciprocate your positive energy. Once you fully commit to healing, you open yourself up a world full of healing agents. You will understand that most people were just instruments in your evolution. You will need to focus on the lesson and the message, not the messenger.

KEY NUMBER FIVE

Repeat this mantra regularly: I am ready to accept extremely positive transformation, abundance, and blessings.

KEY NUMBER SIX

Think of yourself as a human magnet. You are constantly attracting what you speak, think, and feel. Not who you tell people you are, appear to be on social media or even who you believe you are, you will attract what you are. Taking the time to form a better version of yourself is the best investment you can make because you will soon begin to attract greater to you as you become greater.

KEY NUMBER SEVEN

Free your energy. Take these steps to create a high vibrational lifestyle:

    a. Talk to yourself kindly and positively

    b. Challenge yourself daily

    c. Workout and read often

    d. Learn something daily

    e. Create a lifestyle of love around you

    f. Stand up for yourself and your beliefs

    g. Walk away from drama

    h. Express gratitude

    i. Always flow with life

KEY NUMBER EIGHT

Sit in silence and write your goals on a sheet of paper *with a pencil.*Fold that paper and sleep with it under your pillow for a few nights. Wake up, unfold that paper, and reaffirm your goals with the new visions given to you during your slumber. Record your visions and ideas as they come to you even if you don't totally understand their meaning.

KEY NUMBER NINE

Listen to Detox Meditation music at 741 Hz. This helps to remove mental blockages, cleanse aura, and dissolve toxins. This can be found on Youtube or through a Google search. Simply explained, musical tones exist on frequencies and resonate with our minds and bodies. This 741 Hz frequency in particular, can be used to stimulate your mind so thoughts and ideas grounded at the forefront of your mind may give way to other thoughts moving around in the back of your mind. Try it while meditating, planning, cleaning, sleeping, etc.

KEY NUMBER TEN

Find a manifest partner. This is someone you can share your dreams, thoughts, and revelations with. Anytime two people focus on one thing, it manifests twice as fast. This, like all things in life, works much more effectively if both people sincerely believe in themselves and their goals. Accountability is always an important factor.

KEY NUMBER ELEVEN

Repeat these Manifest Affirmations:

a. I am letting go of every part of me that is not contributing to my elevation.

b. I am moving forward with dignity, grace, and patience.

c. I am welcoming this new chapter with the highest level of gratitude and humility.

d. My spirit rises to match the new and magical beginning that awaits me.

e. Low-vibrating energies can't reach me at this height.

f. My vision is locked and focused on the multiple blessings that are coming my way.

CHAPTER TWO

UNDERSTANDINGS
AND OVER-STANDINGS

These are concepts, principles, and truths for you to grasp and apply. Learn these 11 keys. Memorize them like the brightest stars in the night sky; for should you ever get lost in life, you can use these guiding lights to navigate back home.

KEY NUMBER TWELVE

The outer world mirrors the inner world. In order for anything to exist, it must have begun internally. In order for an outward change to occur, the change must happen first internally. Whether we are referencing your mind, your relationship, or your household, what is done within will eventually make an outward appearance.

KEY NUMBER THIRTEEN

Time is the fastest moving currency you have. When time is used correctly your life can feel like an open landscape rather than a fenced in property. Learn to think, operate and invest in a manner that provides you residual returns on your time. Right timing moves things into fruition faster than right choices. Seize your moment viciously when it's ripe. If your time isn't spent on your purpose, people, or position, you are moving unwisely.

KEY NUMBER FOURTEEN

Faith is the strongest currency you possess. Faith can purchase things that are not yet in your possession by willing them into your reality. Relentless belief pushes one beyond the boundaries of reason and logic. Faith is an awareness of connection to your future that is so strong within, that is matters not if the present moment reflects what you believe or not. Faith does not need evidence, if fact faith is its own evidence of a deeper understanding.

KEY NUMBER FIFTEEN

Faith and fear cannot coexist. They won't dwell in the same temple simultaneously. Faith is a positive belief in something for your future and fear is a negative believe in something for you future. You have to choose which one will inhabit it your being. What you feed thrives and what you starve dies! Cheat on your fears. Break up with your doubts. Get engaged to your purpose to marry your dreams.

KEY NUMBER SIXTEEN

Nothing binds you except for your thoughts. Nothing limits you except for your fears. Nothing controls you except for your beliefs.

KEY NUMBER SEVENTEEN

The best math you can learn is the future cost and payout of a current decision.

KEY NUMBER EIGHTEEN

Choose patience and trust in the process. Everything you have visualized, intended, prayed for, and worked for is in the process of manifesting. Remain centered and at peace. Be strong and continue to believe! When manifesting always be specific about what you expect.

KEY NUMBER NINETEEN

There is an evolution in your errors. This is not a race to perfection. You become a better player in sports by missing shots, and in the same way, you become a better person (and a better spiritual being) by missing the mark. You then have the chance to come back to the gym, the court, or the field of life and practice your technique. Take every opportunity to develop yourself through trial-and-error, practice, and persistence. There is magic in your missed shots and mistakes.

KEY NUMBER TWENTY

You are the divine creator of your own reality. If you don't want greatness enough to reject the "good enough" in your life, why would greatness want you? What we settle for is what we are telling the universe we are willing to accept and what we accept is what we are telling the universe we are willing to settle for.

KEY NUMBER TWENTY-ONE

Bad seeds don't lead to good fruit. As we set the tone for atonement, be careful with the works of your being. Do not engage in anger, strife, deception, or dishonesty. Make no mistake about it, situations will arise to test your patience and mindstate. Keep your heart and motives pure. You don't need to be perfect, just consistently aware of each opportunity to welcome positive energy and the ways of your higher self.

KEY NUMBER TWENTY-TWO

Your energy and impact is the most abundant and valuable currency you have. You are the magic. Let's be clear: There are no magic potions or magic words that will transform your life. Knowledge alone is not power; it's the *application* of knowledge in real time that holds power. The practical execution of an understanding is an over-standing, and the effects of operating in over-standings are magnificent. But if you're looking for magic, the best sleight-of-hand trickery you can master is intentionally making the right choices, consecutively, over a span of time, and at such a high rate that you will generate what appears to be the magic of overnight success to those watching from a distance. You can become so crafted and in tune with your gifts that you appear to possess a magical touch and ability!

CHAPTER THREE

SELF-MASTERY

Self - mastery is the longest, most important, and often the most difficult journey we will ever go on. You owe it to yourself to master yourself. If you do not master yourself, you will be mastered *by* self; you will become a daily slave to the desires, fears, addictions, and habits of your lower self. Put these keys to good use. When the enemy within is conquered, the enemy outside stands no chance.

KEY NUMBER TWENTY-THREE

Your health is an investment not an expense. Most successful people start their day taking care of their physical and mental health. Your success will only be as good as your mindset.

KEY NUMBER TWENTY-FOUR

Self-mastery is an uphill battle. But a soldier does not fight because they hate what's in front of them; they fight because they love what's *behind* them. Use your family, history, heritage, and legacy goals as a driving force of motivation and inspiration to conquer every conquest. Understand that you will make mistakes. You will hurt people. Apologize. There is growth in understanding that there are thing you need to work on. Nothing breeds enlightenment like striving for continuous perfection.

KEY NUMBER TWENTY-FIVE

When you know yourself, you are powerful; when you accept yourself, you are invincible. There is something so massively freeing about the acceptance of oneself. It radiates even farther than a beacon of light. Freedom from self-doubt leads to an environment of self-belief. That self-belief produces faith, which is the fuel needed to transport, transcend, and transform one state of your existence to another. You were sent to this dimension as an asset. However, if you do not cultivate your greatness, you will exist in and leave this dimension as a liability, not yielding forth the bountiful harvest you held the potential for.

KEY NUMBER TWENTY-SIX

We repeat what we don't repair in the actions of our lives. As long as we don't acknowledge the break in the system, or the problem in our reality, we are never positioning ourselves to fix it. The term "ignorance is bliss" comes from the concept that if you don't know something, you cannot be held accountable for it. If your aim is to correct something, you must first start by identifying it. You can't heal what you hide. We subconsciously seek situations in which we can act out our old, emotional wounds until we can heal. People have grown old and even gone to their grave still being controlled by their traumas and acting out of unresolved issues and pain. If you do not heal yourself, you will repeat the same patterns.

KEY NUMBER TWENTY-SEVEN

Confront your triggers. The moment you stop looking around and start looking within, you can begin to identify and question your triggers. Then and only then will you see the root of your triggers. Healing is done in layers, and you have to remove layers to heal properly. It's not a beautiful process at all; it is an ugly and lonely process for most of us. But if done correctly and diligently, it will be the best thing you ever do for yourself and your quality of life. You have to accept your emotions, mistakes, and circumstances to change and release them. Without deep inner work, there is no healing, only temporary bandages.

KEY NUMBER TWENTY-EIGHT

Manifesting You **is your first divine purpose and obligation.** You got this. And the ancestors are so proud of every step and stride you take—even the failed attempts! We need you, but no one needs you like YOU need you! Isolation used wisely leads to re-grounding and a clearer focus. Begin to fill your life with pieces of peace. Let go of those who don't treat your soul with care. Forget what you were taught and redesign the landscape of your life one foot at a time if you have to. I promise you are going to look so much better and be so much stronger on the other side. See you there!

KEY NUMBER TWENTY-NINE

Nothing changes until you do. And that shouldn't be problematic! Acceptance of change for your betterment should always be embraced. However, we are creatures of habit, tradition, and cultural conformity. This added to the effects of centuries of psychological warfare and social/economic oppression and conditioning, it seems that the truth of the matter is many of us aren't equipped, resourced, or in an environment to support self-betterment. I say "it seems" because that truth is only as real as you believe and allow it to be. We will deal more with mindset and manifesting the visions of our mind's eye later in this book, but for now, let's begin focusing on your inward image of self, and everything that makes you wonderfully marvelous with power. For some, this may be an introduction to the realm of oneself; for others, it will offer the chance to get reacquainted with oneself.

KEY NUMBER THIRTY

Seek and you will find, then once you grab a hold of your truth, you will begin to rebuild yourself to resemble your new inward identity.You'll task yourself with chipping away at the characteristics or lifestyle choices that no longer are a part of the image you see for yourself. Self-respect will encourage and enforce barriers to protect the glory of you as you fall in love with your raw divinity.

KEY NUMBER THIRTY-ONE

Make peace with yourself, and the rest will fall in line. Let's start here and drop our internal GPS pin by being open and honest about our internal state. I encourage you to write down all you can identify as your strengths, weaknesses, perceptions of self, and desired states of being. Identifying these factors will serve much purpose throughout your journey, much like the legend on a map. This map will lead to a place of milk and honey in the form of a solid and fulfilled state of being. Keep in mind: The shortest distance between two points is a straight line.

KEY NUMBER THIRTY-TWO

Before you can Master an enemy, you must know its name. There are 6 main fears commonly the reason most don't reach for their greatness. Do you fear any of these?

a. Poverty

b. Criticism

c. Loss of health

d. Loss of love

e. Fear of old age

f. Death

As I previously mentioned, faith and fear cannot coexist so if any of these items are present in your life or mind, you must activate the tools to destroy your fear and build your faith.

KEY NUMBER THIRTY-THREE

Refuse anger. The aggressive person is normally the one who has the least control. When making aggressive movements, you can only see three or four steps ahead. You often cannot make wise long-term choices when acting through aggression. The calmest person in the room normally has the most power. And since much power is based on perception, remaining collected and poised reflects that you are in complete control of the situation and unbothered by it. An ancient African proverb says, *"An angry heart is mad at its owner."*

KEY NUMBER THIRTY-FOUR

Indecision, doubt and fear are three enemies you must confront and conquer. This trio will not only distract and misdirect you but also lowers the frequency on which you operate. You must know them to be your enemies because they rival the feelings, emotions and thought patterns that would lead to your health, success and obtainment of your desires. Indecision is the seedling of fear. It crystallizes into doubt. The two mixed together form fear. Nothing is created without an impulse of thought so make up your mind and move accordingly.

KEY NUMBER THIRTY-FIVE

An honest self-assessment is required for daily alignment. This practice keeps you on the correct course as the tides and waves of life push and pull you in various directions. This doesn't require a total unpacking, but you should keep in mind that we manage what we measure. Self-management must be your first priority because you are your most lucrative asset. As such, never allow yourself to be internally compromised for long. Honesty is the stairway to peace. Once obtained, if you are wise enough to protect your peace, your peace will guide and protect you in return. It's not until you are rooted in your truths that you can become ruthless in your demands. Flaws and all, be unashamed when you put your state of being on a scale and weigh where you are at mentally, spiritually, and emotionally. After you take time for self-reflection and identification, you can now start the engine with the keys to acquire the knowledge of the self, the utilization of self-respect, and the administration of a healthy dose of self-love. When you love yourself better; you will attract better. You will let yourself and the universe know that you deserve the best by treating yourself well. Everything starts with how you feel about yourself—so feel worthy, valuable, special, and deserving!

KEY NUMBER THIRTY-SIX

Give yourself to yourself. Every new day is the greatest opportunity you've ever had to be greater than you've ever been. To maximize your potential, each day should start before the demands of your life require your focus. Begin with a period of silence and observation before planning and problem-solving. Before the kids wake up, before the spouse needs you, before getting back to whatever you didn't finish yesterday, before you give yourself to anything else—GIVE YOURSELF TO YOURSELF. No phone, no TV, no radio, no outside opinions or agendas, no frequency other than your own. Let that permeate. Self-discipline is one of the greatest expressions of self-love. Putting off an immediate desire for a long-term benefit is as real as love gets.

KEY NUMBER THIRTY-SEVEN

Get out of your mind, get into your soul.
Meditation helps tap into the limitless dimension of
your existence. As beings comprised of soul, mind,
and body we live simultaneously on 3 separate
planes of existence: They are known and referred to
as: The great physical plain, the great mental plane,
and the great spiritual plane. The universal
law/principle of correspondence exclaims there can
always be a harmony obtained between all 3 planes.
This not only means your mind, body, and soul can
operate in alignment, but other things in each
corresponding plane can work to and for your
benefit as well.

KEY NUMBER THIRTY-EIGHT

In a very spiritual way, connect with the part of you that isn't weighed down by your present reality. This connection pulls your concentration outside the realm of your present needs and responsibilities. Elevate your mind to see above the circumstantial mountains that may be prohibiting your best point of view. Be very intentional to avoid what distracts you from your time of solitude and daybreak devotions. More gold has been mined from the minds of men than from any other place on the planet, so follow your light into the quarry of your being with great anticipation, looking to see what precious minerals are waiting to be polished. Connect with your soul and write down its goals.

KEY NUMBER THIRTY-NINE

Personal accountability requires mindfulness, acceptance, and courage. The best thing I ever did to change my life was begin to dig deep and ask myself why I am the way I am and do the things I do. Getting to know yourself on a deeper level will help you thrive (on your own and with others). Self evaluation and personal development is self care at its best. Your mindset and actions should be the product of heart and goals, not your environment. You can either allow your Higher self to evolve you or your lower self to rob you. Make a verbal commitment to your goals and purpose daily. This is a great way to center yourself in what truly matters most and realize what is otherwise a distraction.

KEY NUMBER FORTY

Elevation calls for isolation. When you raise your vibration, all that is not in alignment with you will naturally leave your life. As your frequency rise you would no longer feel the desire to follow Trends and fit in. Authenticity is a huge factor in your growth and evolution. You'll know you are truly on your path when being yourself and honoring who you truly are becomes a priority.

KEY NUMBER FORTY-ONE

If you don't deal with your pain, it will form a mental prison you will be forced to deal with. I'm confident you have witnessed an adult behave in a rather immature or childish way when they were confronted with an issue they did not want to or know how to handle. This occurs because one does not mature past an unhealed point of pain. When a current scenario brushes up against an old wound, the person often acts out of the same mindset they were in when the wound was originally received. It could be a childhood trauma that was triggered and pulled the grownup back into adolescent conduct. A present day conversation can scrape the scab of a cut from a past relationship and the person's reaction comes from the previous place of pain, not the real time situation. I know personally, I couldn't heal in certain areas of my life because I kept pretending, I wasn't hurt.

KEY NUMBER FORTY-TWO

Forgiveness sets you free. Unforgiveness grants permission to harbor negative thoughts and emotions. It's eager to justify not progressing beyond a circumstance. This will only keep you bound and unable to move through life freely. I will admit, I have been that person before. In moments, I was completely unaware I was acting out of old pain I still had not forgiven someone for. Even if someone has wronged you, refusing to forgive them is no different than choosing to take a new sip of their old poison everyday, whether they offered you a drink or not.

KEY NUMBER FORTY-THREE

Reclaim your strength with these 5 steps on how to outgrow your triggers:

1. When you feel it coming, take a step back and breathe. Pause yourself and assess the direction of your mind and what feeling or memory is connected to the present moment.

2. Observe (don't react) even though this will feel highly uncomfortable.

3. Re-program the subconscious. Affirm: "I am grateful for the emotion and what it can teach me."

4. You will form a new relationship with the emotion after examining it carefully. Find its root cause. You will be disconnecting the emotion from the trauma and associating it with what the situation offers you to learn from.

5. Let go and continue progressing

KEY NUMBER FORTY-FOUR

Set yourself on fire. From childhood to present day, I've had an infatuation with fire. Its boldness and honesty is irrefutable. It rarely tells a lie, nor will it accept yours. I can relate. In fact, at around age six or seven, as a fire burned down my home, I still thought it was amazing to marvel at the massive flames roaring down the stairway, as though they preceded some angry dungeon dragon. Starting a physical fire is still one of my favorite things to do, but I consider it to be a big-time blessing when I get to ignite a fire within people. I've witnessed a spark in someone's mind become a flame, and that flame combusted into a blaze, and that blaze grew until others, near and far, knew of its existence. That's golden. I believe you are golden, as well, and it's time to throw an entire can of whatever fuels you onto your thoughts and desires, like gasoline on dry wood. Fire is known as a purifying agent. Even the few things that are capable of temporarily coexisting with it—such as gold and silver—are refined (i.e., purified) in its presence. The metals melt, and impurities are skimmed away. You see, fire requires a change of form. The power and cleansing ability of fire has been used and referenced all throughout time and countless cultures. The overwhelming power of fire has always been conveyed to you, whether it was from the idea of a fire burning in one's soul to achieve what seems impossible, or the story of Sodom and Gomorrah from the Bible, Torah, and Quran, wherein the cities of sin were destroyed with brimstone and fire sent from God. It only took one or two incidents with fire before you instinctually understood that, once initiated, a fire could destroy anything that was not created to withstand its unapologetic behavior. Fire asks for no permissions to thrive in its created purpose. Fire gives no fucks about bystanders, onlookers, structures, previous agendas, or future plans. "GET YOUR ASS OUT OF MY WAY!" fire screams at anything dumb cnough to stand in its path. When reaching for and operating within your created purpose, you have to move with the same audacious tenacity. You will disrupt preexisting conditions when your fire is set ablaze. Some familiar objects and ideas will get burnt in the process, but each destruction is the beginning of a new life. Your fire will make way for itself to progress, the same way a natural fire sends its heat to dry out new ground so that it can advance. Flames are intensified when the combustion rate is increased. In this case, "combustion" is your productivity and hard work. The more efficiently you work on/for your created purpose, the more it will work on/for you. Set yourself on fire.

CHAPTER FOUR

KNOWLEDGE OF SELF

Every day, extraordinary lives are abandoned and stolen because their value was not recognized. Just as I've seen the viciousness of my brothers killing each other in cold blood, I've observed a man give up his own potency and potential and waste his life away one day at a time. I ask you: Who is more at fault? The man who took a life in one action or moment? Or the man who sealed his fate every day? Self-knowledge, self-respect, and self-love are the tools to renovate, renew, and increase your life's property value.

KEY NUMBER FORTY-FIVE

Knowledge of self creates love of self. Love of self demands respect of self. I heard Derrick Grace II say something along those lines one day and it made so much sense. He went on to explain how so many of our destructive behaviors exist due to a lack of self-love and respect that our people have not obtained because they have no knowledge of the self. The subject matter around this sidewalk conversation was our culture's eating habits. He closed by pointing out how willingly we pay for premium gas for our luxury cars because we want the best performance and value for our vehicle, but we will simultaneously fuel ourselves with the cheapest/unhealthiest food sources offered because we don't properly see the value in ourselves. Respect and value go hand-in-hand.

KEY NUMBER FORTY-SIX

When you consider something expensive and of value, you treat it with the degree of care required to be kept in that condition. It's your perception of something's value that gives it value. Make the choice today to perceive yourself to be a priceless and a rare commodity. Very few people in life will ever hold you at a higher regard than you hold yourself. That is why you must know your value and stand firmly on it. Demand every cent of want you deserve for your time, knowledge and the experience your presence provides. Know your worth, add tax, plus interest and don't budge. If they can't pay the toll, they can't cross the bridge.

KEY NUMBER FORTY-SEVEN

If there was ever a time to bet it all on yourself, it's right now. Self-knowledge, self-respect, and self-love are the tools you need to renovate, renew, and increase the value of your life. It is time to connect with the divine purpose and power that exists within you. Doing so will allow you to manifest things in this dimension, which is what you were sent here to do. Take the steps to identify all your alignments, attributes, and righteous weaponry to make yourself powerful.

KEY NUMBER FORTY-EIGHT

You are only limited to who and what you believe you are. You can only have and do what you believe you can. The image you hold of yourself and the image you have of yourself is the foundation on which you base your capabilities and limitations. You design your own box depending on the faith level of your imagination. In all things and at all times find yourself to be greater than whatever you find yourself fighting because your mind believes what you tell it.

KEY NUMBER FORTY-NINE

Find beautiful pictures of where you've come from, historical places of people who look like you. Enlighten and uplift your mind with images that glorify your historical royalty and reign on this earth. Whether you choose to dig into your family history or ancient history, take the time to familiarize yourself with the greatness you descend from. Study the greats and their ambitions. History has a way of inspiring the future. Dive into the power that predates you and harness it.

KEY NUMBER FIFTY

To manufacture the best version of yourself, you must first confront the *current* version of yourself.You must consider many of the traits that make up your personality and identity which were given to you throughout your life by the environments that you came from. Belief systems and entire schools of thought, behaviors and behavioral patterns, reactive instincts, defense mechanisms, and even coping mechanisms were all either developed by you or instilled in you by others or your surroundings. Like the rest of nature, these ways of existence are often techniques to survive the realities of your environment, as well as the traumas that you endure. It is important to take time to identify some of the character traits that you should abandon. Exhibiting old ways in a new season can be very detrimental.

KEY NUMBER FIFTY-ONE

Ask yourself these six questions to begin your voyage into a mental space of not reacting to the limitations of your environment:

   a. Who am I outside of the identity that pain has given me?

   b. What would I be like if my past experiences didn't "make me this way?"

   c. If money wasn't an issue, what would I do every day based on my love for it?

   d. What would I like to *not* be afraid of?

   e. How would I love if I felt free to express it?

   f. What do people tell me I am gifted or great at that I have yet to seriously pursue?

KEY NUMBER FIFTY-TWO

In a very spiritual way, connect with the part of you that isn't weighted by your present reality. This connection pulls your concentration outside the realm of your present needs and responsibilities and tunes you into the part of you that exists far beyond the 3 dimensions of your physical world. You will begin to feel free as this connection strengthens. You will notice an elevated point of view and a perspective based off higher trains of thought.

KEY NUMBER FIFTY-THREE

It's time to unwrap another layer and identify some desires, goals, and passions, and dreams we abandoned due to circumstances, lack of time and/or resources. On a sheet of paper write down "soul's goals" on one side and "heart's passions" on the other. Start a list of things that set fire to your soul when you think about them.

KEY NUMBER FIFTY-FOUR

Never allow yourself to be internally compromised for long. Honesty is the stairway to peace. Once obtained, if you are wise enough to protect your peace, your peace will guide and protect you. This is where boundaries come into play. Protect your peace at all costs.

KEY NUMBER FIFTY-FIVE

Awaken your authenticity. Let's find what I call "purpose points." These are exercises that help point you towards your purpose.

a. Remember what you liked to do as a kid.

b. Identify what you would love to do if money wasn't an issue.

c. Think about the talents and skillsets that you have and can utilize right now which don't involve traveling or much assistance from anyone else.

d. Imagine that you have no obligations, and things don't have to "make sense." You are free to make any choice you'd like. What comes to mind?

e. Think like a child. Come from the heart and start doing what your heart tells you to do with the resources you have available right now.

f. What do you imagine yourself doing that's so big, it scares you? Do that! Fate loves the fearless. If you feel energized by the possibility—even though it's terrifying—then that's a strong sign you should pursue it.

g. What same opportunity keeps coming to you in different ways, forms, and versions? This is an opportunity that may come unprovoked in conversations—even with strangers! Again, this is a strong sign you should pursue it.

h. Stimulate your purpose points for 30 minutes a day.

KEY NUMBER FIFTY-SIX

You have to believe in yourself beyond what your current situation or environment tells you. You have to see yourself and your future reality within your mind's eye and your heart of hearts. You have to know it like you know your name. You have to believe in it like the air you breathe.

KEY NUMBER FIFTY-SEVEN

It's time to point out all of the magnificent things that make you wonderfully marvelous. Believe it or not your superpower lies within these abilities, skill sets, mindset, and unique characteristics that make you a one of one. Even your scars show what could not break you. This is the moment to find beauty even in your flaws. You're perfectly imperfect and now is the time to give yourself permission to love you apologetically. Be unashamed when you put your state of being on a scale and weigh out where you are at mentally, spiritually, and emotionally. Understand that these stats aren't edged in stone. Reinvent yourself and rewrite the story of your life at will. Take yourself on a date. Truly enjoy your presence and reconnect with your inner love life.

KEY NUMBER FIFTY-EIGHT

Make peace with yourself and the rest will fall in line. Never allow yourself to be internally compromised for long. Un-compromised honesty with yourself is the stairway to inner peace. Once obtained, if you are wise enough to protect your peace, your peace will guide and protect you. *It's not until you are rooted in your truths that you can become ruthless in your demands.*

KEY NUMBER FIFTY-NINE

Set boundaries around yourpeace. Implement self-care into your daily regimen. Boundaries protect; a lack of boundaries invites a lack of respect. The only ones who would not want to respect your boundaries are those who secretly intend to disrespect your space. Setting boundaries is an everyday action item for self-care and self-respect.

KEY NUMBER SIXTY

Use your sixth sense and see with your third eye. There is an undeniable sixth sense that we all share. You may be unfamiliar with it by name or understanding, but you have undoubtedly lived a life experiencing it. Although its existence and abilities are recognized, it's not accounted for alongside the other five senses that are acknowledged by the medical and psychological communities because modern schools of thought cannot link it to any of the organs previously declared for use by sensory functions. But you don't need man's science to accept your divine reality. You can close your eyes right now and see your past, as well as your future. Think about it: You can see with your eyes closed! So, where is the third eye that provides vision without physical sight? Your sixth sense manifests in the form of mental visions, foresight, premonitions, knowledge, and understandings that are not rooted in something that you have already been taught, the event referred to as "Déjà vu," and other moments of mental clarity beyond one's conscious realm of understanding. This additional boundless sight comes from an organ the size of a grain of rice, located deep in the center of your brain, called the "pineal gland" or "epiphysiscerebri." It is commonly referred to as the "third eye" or your "mind's eye."

From sleeping patterns to the way one perceives reality, your pineal gland affects decision making and even psychological development.

The presence of your sixth sense has been known as:

a. Intuition;

b. Intuitive spirit;

c. Holy Spirit;

d. Inner unconsciousness;

e. The god mind/god state;

f. Divine universal connection; and/or

g. Universal mind.

Whatever you like to call it, this additional sensory ability can and will warn you of impending danger in time for you to avoid it, as well as alert you to great opportunity in time for you to seize it. Western religion and philosophy have done a miraculous job of steering us away from the acknowledgement and use of this powerful line of sight. This gland, its functions, and its powerful benefits are essential for a strong, indigenous mind and body. If it were not, it wouldn't be under such chemical attacks from the European powers-that-be. Fluoride placed in our water, toothpaste, and other products that we use daily is the dominant cause of calcification of the pineal gland. This hardens the tissue of the gland with calcium, much like when your skin becomes callused.

Less melatonin is produced which affects which affects sleep cycles, your mental state, hormone balance, menstrual cycle, fertility, and other important lifecycles.

CHAPTER FIVE

HABITS

Success, failure, wealth, poverty, sickness, and health are all obtained through regularly repeated routines and behaviors. So, no matter what the landscape of your life looks like, the power of your habits can and most likely will determine what it will *continue* to look like, creating either the life you want or the life you don't. You now have the keys; what will you do with them? To get something that you never had; you will have to do something you have never done. Keep climbing; I'll meet you at the top!

KEY NUMBER SIXTY-ONE

Your habits are the framework of your life. When dealing with habits, there can be no compromise between your actions and your desired outcome just as there is no compromise between poverty and riches or happiness and sadness . The roads that lead to them flow into completely different directions and under two completely different currents. If you want riches you must abandon every road that leads to poverty. This far exceeds the realm of finances. I'm not really referring to material possessions and the accumulation of money at all, but rather riches in terms of wealth of Life, happiness, spirituality, prosperity and peace. Obtaining the best version of YOU is real bag!

KEY NUMBER SIXTY-TWO

Great achievements are usually born from great sacrifice and are almost never the child of greed. The universe works in such a divine way and purposeful order, that even the events that appear to be luck are in fact usually the result of proper habits. Habits have no moral standard or opinion. They could be good or bad. They don't care. Your habits are formed by repetitive thoughts and repetitive supportive actions.

KEY NUMBER SIXTY-THREE

Your habits either grant your dreams permission to grow and manifest, or they are the reason your aspirations will struggle to breathe—and eventually, cease to exist. There are plenty of examples around you of good and bad habits, and the results they yield. Once you decide what you want, you must examine your daily routine and habits. Identify what is creating a bridge to your promise land and what is creating a barrier around where you are currently.

KEY NUMBER SIXTY-FOUR

As powerful as your habits are; you have complete power over them. Ask yourself: What does what you do today have to say about your tomorrow? What do your habits have to say about your future? Where are your habits leading you? Better yet—what could you start doing today to get your lifestyle more aligned with your desired destination?

KEY NUMBER SIXTY-FIVE

Goal-setting and detailed planning are the basis of every achievement, so your habits are either a daily step forward or backward. Habits have destinations attached to them. Your habits form your realities by building bridges between your present existence, where you want to go, and where you would rather not be. Where are your habits taking you?

KEY NUMBER SIXTY-SIX

If you understand, then you over-stand. Knowledge is great, but *applied knowledge* is even greater. After grasping a principle, you must put it into action immediately. This will lead to the formation of new habits that regularly support your new understanding and goals. An over-standing is an understanding applied in real time. An over-standing is the actionable item based on your understand. It's simple: "Now that I know this, I don't do that."

KEY NUMBER SIXTY-SEVEN

Small alignments lead to big adjustments. When it comes to navigation, staying on course is constant obligation if you wish to reach your desired destination in a timely manner. Any pilot or captain will tell you the slightest directional change, uncorrected over time will lead to a vastly different destination than what was planned. This principle works in your favor as well since even small alignments lead to big adjustments. As you navigate your life's journey, whether through the smooth heaven kissed skies or the rough wayward seas, making seemingly small changes to your routines, habits, diets, words, thoughts, mental processing, etc. will align your internal compass with mapping to transport and transform your life in a major way. Traveling through life bares much resemblance to the act of traveling itself. Once the trajectory is set, momentum and time will get you to your desired destination.

KEY NUMBER SIXTY-EIGHT

Kill your killer habits. From how we delegate our time to how we manage our finances and diets; we will continue to experience the same symptoms and illnesses if we do not fix the detrimental habits that cause the unfavorable conditions we wish to escape. Diseases don't run in the family; they run in the eating habits. Poverty is a mindset that is rooted in a lack of financial literacy and supported by bad financial habits.

KEY NUMBER SIXTY-NINE

Turn your "should-dos" into "must-dos". Once your habits are aligned with a specific goal or purpose, you will have the building blocks and stepping stones to get you to the next milestone achievement along your path. Time is nonrefundable; distribute it accordingly.

KEY NUMBER SEVENTY

As powerful as your habits are, you have complete power over them. Avoid being the type of person who:

a. makes excuses or waits until later to do things;

b. communicates poorly;

c. lacks the emotional maturity to handle opposing opinions without getting angered;

d. does not like accountability;

e. says they want one thing, but their actions contradict their desires;

f. wants a healthy body but fills themselves with unhealthy food;

g. desires a healthy relationship yet displays toxic behavior;

h. always needs more money but spends unnecessarily; and/or

i. wastes time with unproductive pastimes.

KEY NUMBER SEVENTY-ONE

Discipline is the strongest form of self-love. Discipline is intentional decision-making backed by supportive actions. Discipline is ignoring the current pleasures of the mind and body for the greater future reward or desire. Not to mention that your words become more powerful when your actions back them up. Sometimes, after meditating on a desire or intention to obtain something, you will come across an opportunity that bears the appearance of whatever you were meditating on. Two things are happening here: (1) the law of attraction is working for you; and (2) the universe/God/divine powers have gifted you with an opportunity to exercise your faith, intentions, and habits on what you decide. Don't waste this chance! Respond to them without hesitation!

CHAPTER SIX

ASSETS AND ALLIES

Relationships are an important part of your ascension and must be used strategically. As the designer of your destiny, you must be careful who you allow near you. If your connections aren't going in the direction you desire for your life, then you aren't, either. Your new understandings and over-standings will make some people uncomfortable. It may even provoke anger in those who do not wish to elevate themselves or change their circumstances. Fuck 'em! People mistake the truth for disrespect because *it disrespects the lie they mistake for the truth*. But here's a reminder: We didn't come on this journey to make or keep friends. As a matter of fact, when it comes to people in your life, less is more, my friend. If they aren't lifting you up, they are weighing you down. If they aren't pushing you forward, they are pulling you back. Not anymore! Grab a broom! This is your spring cleaning and soul cleansing. Go right ahead and clear the clutter and purge; throw away some people!

KEY NUMBER SEVENTY-TWO

Assess your assets. Your family, friends, coworkers, and social communities make up your network of allies and assets. People around you possess trades, skill sets, or even personality traits that can be used to your benefit. Your net worth is a byproduct of your network. People provide connections that often lead to shortcuts. Furthermore, whatever they are good should be seen as a valuable tool that may be a great benefit to you. Now is a good time to look over your network of people and identify a few people who appear to have similar goals as you. These may be individuals you can team up with or at least learn from. Keep an open eye and mind. It's easy to overlook a great candidate and/or miss a divine opportunity because you were expecting it to be packaged a certain way. Learn the language of leverage.

KEY NUMBER SEVENTY-THREE

Eliminate toxic connections. Unhealthy attachments are a fast way to drain yourself of time, energy, and resources.Stop feeding people who just want a plate to go and build with the ones who want to see you grow. If you see people by their actions, you will never be fooled by their words. Learn the difference between connection and attachment. Connection gives you power; attachment *uses* your power.

KEY NUMBER SEVENTY-FOUR

Codependency is a crutch. Self-reliance is a must. When you depend on someone to feed you, you give them the power to starve you. A codependent relation forms unhealthy bonds and habits. This is excessive emotional or psychological reliance on a partner. Inability to set boundaries, believe that you are responsible for someones emotions, fear of speaking the truth, lowering self worth, fear of rejection, and absorbing the emotional state of another by default are all strong symptoms of codependency.

KEY NUMBER SEVENTY-FIVE

Don't let people walk through your mind with their dirty feet. You certainly wouldn't allow someone to walk across your bed tracking outside dirt all through the area you lay your head so take the same approach when it comes to what you allow others to traffic through your head. Some words and conversations aren't to be allowed the opportunity to dwell in your mind or take root in your belief system. Learn to release any negative words spoken to you, over you, or about you that is unwanted or unyielding to your peace.

KEY NUMBER SEVENTY-SIX

Staff your weakness. You can maximize your potential by focusing on the areas you are the strongest/most powerful in, soliciting the help of someone dominant in the area(s) you are weak in. Surround yourself with people who are fluent in your weak areas. This is an ultimate life hack.

KEY NUMBER SEVENTY-SEVEN

No squares in the circle. For this principle, I want you to imagine a circle around you and your team/staff/supporters. This is your circle. Everyone in the circle should be on one accord and working towards one collective goal. For the sake of illustration, we will refer to anyone who is not attached to your purpose or supporting your goals as a "square." You will need to remove them from your immediate circle. They simply don't fit in this particular realm of your life. Although it may be uncomfortable to transition away from some of your favorite squares, it's absolutely necessary for your growth and forward progression.

KEY NUMBER SEVENTY-EIGHT

What's meant for you won't be toxic. What's meant for you will not require you to water yourself down, dumb yourself down, or give others a "diet" version of yourself. What's meant for you should never be confused with what's *available* to you. People lose what they should have because they settle for what they *can* have. Ask yourself: Is it pulling you or fueling you? Pay close attention to who and what causes your energy to increase and decrease. The universe gives you plenty of hints about whom you should embrace. With a toxic partner, a disagreement will turn into an argument, which will lead to a bigger problem. With a divine partner, a disagreement will turn into a conversation, which will lead to a solution. Accept no substitutes. Anyone in your life who does not present the attributes of an asset is more than likely a liability waiting to happen. Deal with them accordingly—if you must deal with them at all. The name of the game has always been to minimize the liabilities in your life. No exceptions, no excuses. If you live by this rule, you will live a better life. Avoid people who:

a. are unable to apologize sincerely on their own;

b. act like the victim when confronted with their actions/abusive/toxic behavior;

c. expect you to prioritize them but don't prioritize you;

d. mess with your head;

e. intentionally or repeatedly do/say things which they know upset you; and/or

f. take offense when you hold them accountable.

Anapology without changed behavior is nothing more than clever manipulation

KEY NUMBER SEVENTY-NINE

A person seldomly elevates if the people around them always justify their negative behavior. You can't change the people around you but you can change the people around you. The wrong relationship(s) can undo all of the self care work you've been practicing lately. Just say no.

KEY NUMBER EIGHTY

People will always fail to live up to a position/title they should not have been given. Make less decisions based on the potential you see in others, and more based on the fruit of their labors. Also, stop disconnecting with yourself to connect with others.Instead vibrate higher and challenge those around you to elevate.

KEY NUMBER EIGHTY-ONE

An apology without changed behavior is nothing more than clever manipulation.

Avoid people who:

a. are unable to apologize sincerely on their own;

b. act like the victim when confronted with their actions/abusive/toxic behavior;

c. expect you to prioritize them but don't prioritize you;

d. mess with your head;

e. intentionally or repeatedly do/say things which they know upset you; and/or

f. take offense when you hold them accountable.

KEY NUMBER EIGHTY-TWO

When you love yourself you glow from within? You will attract people who love, respect, and appreciate your light. Everything starts with how you fell about yourself. Start feeling worthy, valuable and deserving or receiving the best thatlife has to offer.

KEY NUMBER EIGHTY-THREE

Some of your friendships are trauma bonds. That's why they don't support your elevation Your growth means they can't emotionally attach to your weakness anymore. See it for the toxic connection it is. If it doesn't nourish your soul, let it go. Some people deserve an explanation, some deserve an answer, others deserve absolutely nothing. Begin to distinguish who is who. The best thing you can do is set boundaries that allow you to grow and lead by example. A rising tides raises all boats.

KEY NUMBER EIGHTY-FOUR

The person who challenges you and holds your accountable loves you more than the person that watches you stay the same and settle for mediocrity. Remove yourself from people who treat you like your time like it doesn't matter, like your feelings are worthless, or like your soul is replaceable. If you have a toxic relationship with yourself, your other relationships will be a reflection of it.

CHAPTER SEVEN

THE POWER OF
YOUR WORDS

By now, the way you speak about yourself or your life should have begun to change because your knowledge, opinion, and self-image should have begun to change. As you are now tapping into your power, you should begin training with one of your strongest weapons: your mouth! Your preschool teacher was a witch, and she taught you to cast spells! By definition, a *spell* is a spoken word or form of words having power; a strong, compelling influence or attraction. Simply put and understood, words cast spells! Don't believe me? When you were a kid, you learned a system of placing letters together and uttering their compounded sounds to form a word. That system is known as "spelling". You then learned to put words and their meanings together to vocally express your inward desires for the purpose of impressing them upon others. That sounds like some good ole fashion spellbinding to me! From the very beginning, you were taught to use your words to dictate your environment and life experience. At much earlier stages of life, you imagined (or most assuredly knew!) that screaming your desires could summon their physical manifestation. You understood the power in your vocal expressions. Let's get back to that! (Minus the childhood dramatics and screaming. Ain't nobody got time for that!)

KEY NUMBER EIGHTY-FIVE

Sound is vibration. When you speak, your words omit vibrations and those vibrations, like every other, attract their physical likeness.

KEY NUMBER EIGHTY-SIX

Loose lips sink ships. Think of the biggest boat you've ever seen or been on. Recall its magnificent size and impressive craftsmanship. Now, consider the rudder of the ship. It's one of the smallest pieces of this grand design, yet it controls the entire directional movement of the vessel. Your tongue works the same way. Its size is but an illusion compared to its power and control. The words you speak and allow to be spoken to you can and most likely will direct your life. They are the blueprint to life. You believe what you say, and your subconscious mind can believe what it hears as truth after hearing it enough.

KEY NUMBER EIGHTY-SEVEN

A poor mouth begets a poor life. Many don't realize how they prophesied their most recent flat tire when they previously stated, "If it's not one thing, it's another." Not even taking a chance to realize they are speaking negativity into their path; they meet and greet the current unfortunate circumstance with the powerful declaration, "Bad things always happen to me!" I've seen people with an undoubtable superpower for conjuring up whirlwinds and shitstorms with their proclamations, but they never try to apply the same technique in reverse. Some are so quick to speak negatively about their own children, as though they don't see the power of their words working all around them. If you could see your words manifesting and coming to life in front of you in real time, you would consider your words wisely. Yet we speak words that sow seeds we would never want to grow. At some point, you're going to have to deal with that harvest. This could mean a loss of time, money, or opportunity— or even worse, a loss of wellbeing, love, or life.

KEY NUMBER EIGHTY-EIGHT

Only speak what you want to manifest. Speak on what you desire often. Speak it as if it is currently happening and it will begin to happen. Speak with an expectancy and unwavering faith every time you speak on your dreams and desires. When faced with a problem, speak your solution. Words, when spoken out loud, transform into frequencies and vibrations that can be used to direct energy.

KEY NUMBER EIGHTY-NINE

Use these daily affirmations:

a. Today is a great day!

b. My life is fulfilling, and my business is growing every day!

c. My income increases daily.

d. My peace increases daily.

e. My ability to navigate around the distractions of life increases daily.

f. I love, and I am deeply loved. I give, and I am blessed to receive.

g. People go out of their way to do good things for me.

h. I am so grateful.

i. My children are blessed.

j. I am the divine creator of my reality.

CHAPTER EIGHT

THOUGHTS AND MINDSET

No poison can kill positive thoughts. No medicine can heal negative thoughts. Your thoughts, philosophy, attitude, and perception will determine whether you are met with obstacles or opportunities to perfect your character and abilities.

KEY NUMBER NINETY

Your thoughts are the infrastructure of your life. Your thoughts are the only thing you can almost completely control if you choose to do so. By replacing negative thoughts with positive ones that you consistently and consciously reaffirm to yourself, you can then begin to alter your thoughts and thereby have the ability to change behavior patterns, uprooting one and planting a new one that is in alignment with your desired destination.

KEY NUMBER NINETY-ONE

Our internal dialogue creates the base and foundation on which we build our desires, words, habits, behaviors, intentions, and goals. Think of yourself in good ways. Don't think or speak negative things about yourself, not even as a joke. Your subconscious will not know what to weed out and will accept your bad perception of self as a true reality.

KEY NUMBER NINETY-TWO

The first change that must take place is in your mind. You have to change your mind before you can change the way you're living and the way you move. To change your habits, change your thoughts. To change your thoughts, change your words and beliefs.

KEY NUMBER NINETY-THREE

The power of perception. In all aspects of life, and especially in the wild, daily survival is based off perception. On both a small and extremely large scale, perception determines if you are seen as a potential predator, an equal, or possible prey. In the same way, magic happens when you redirect your thoughts to what you desire rather than what you don't.

KEY NUMBER NINETY-FOUR

Your attitude and perception of your realities determines whether what you are faced with opposition or an opportunity. The way you perceive yourself and your abilities will be the reasoning you use to determine how to handle life as it comes your way. Does this wall require you to turn around and find another route or can you climb over it and keep going?

KEY NUMBER NINETY-FIVE

You are your biggest problem, and your biggest solution. You are the only problem you will ever have, and the only solution you will ever need. You won't see problems the same once you realize that only 10% of your life experience is what happens to you, and the dominant 90% how you react to it. It isn't about the storm; it's about what you do when it forms. Train your mind to see the solutions and look for possible corrective actions. Problem solving is more of a mentality that turns into a skillset because it initiates the presence of a solution rather than the existence of a problem.

KEY NUMBER NINETY-SIX

Victim or Victor? When you realize and accept that nothing is happening to you—rather, everything is happening *for* you—a shift takes place. This shift in mentality allows you to open your heart, mind, and soul to the benefit (present or future) that any given situation has to offer you. A closed mind doesn't get fed either. Accept your past without regret. Handle your present with confidence and face your future without fear.

KEY NUMBER NINETY-SEVEN

Destroy negative thoughts as soon as they enter your mind. That is when they are at their weakest and looking for signs from your life or other thoughts that may support them. You can't fight a thought with a thought. You must fight and defeat a thought with your words. By audibly speaking that which cancels and voids out whatever negative idea or situation may have formed in your mind, you can quiet the negative and reaffirm the positive. Do this immediately before the seed gets a chance to take root in the field of your mind.

KEY NUMBER NINETY-EIGHT

You will attract what's on your mind. You will become what you constantly think about. Once you realize that what you think about expands, you will become much more than you are, and you will start to be really careful of what you think about. When you connect tangible realities to your thought patterns, you won't allow your thoughts to be about anything you don't want to manifest in your life.

CHAPTER NINE

ENERGY

If you think you're too good for certain situations, you are! Emotional energy is neutral; they become "positive" or negative by our feelings, sensations, and physiological reactions. This is why an exciting encounter fell like it gives us fuel and an emotionally exhausting interaction can leave us feeling tired or worn out. Be selective and treat your energy and time with as much care as your finances. Cultivate a sensitivity and awareness of the energy you're emitting and encountering on a daily basis. Assess and implement practical tools to allow you to remain grounded and balanced.

KEY NUMBER NINETY-NINE

Energy is your most valuable currency. You must guard and protect it like a family heirloom. Your energy is one of the most sacred things you have and the most powerful thing you possess. It can calm troubled waters or capsize your life's vessel. Your energy can purchase opportunities your wallet can't. Wasted energy can be more expensive than wasted money. Your energy can gain you favor and otherwise undeserved access to people, places and things you otherwise would be restricted from. A man who walks in purpose doesn't have to chase people or opportunities. The right ones pursue him.

KEY NUMBER ONE HUNDRED

Stop pimping and prostituting your energy. Refrain from taking your energy to places and people in exchange for minimal short-term gains. There is so much value in your energy and the byproducts of it. Walk in the over-standing that you reserve all rights to save, protect, and even charge top dollar for your energy as you deem necessary. Surround yourself with people that reflect who you want to be and how you want to feel. Energy is contagious.

KEY NUMBER ONE HUNDRED ONE

Great mindsets, attitudes, ambition, and intentions are attributes that attract greater relationships, resources and gateways to further your path. Keep your mental state elevated and reflecting exactly what you want out of your moment, day, week, month, season, year, life, and legacy. When you "pay" attention to something, you're buying an experience. It's an investment so "spend" carefully, and only on things that will bring you a good return.

KEY NUMBER ONE HUNDRED TWO

Nothing has ever happened without intention. Goal-setting and detailed planning are the basis of every achievement. Add faith and actions behind a made-up mind, and sooner or later, you'll find an unstoppable momentum. Take inventory of how you delegate your attention. Put energy into the things that fill you up and gives you balance.

KEY NUMBER ONE HUNDRED THREE

Pay attention to what you pay attention to. Attention is energy. What you think about, you bring about. Never let your mind rest on negative ideas, or anything that is counterproductive to your life plan. Where your mind goes, your energy flows. Everything is energy. Your thoughts begin it. Your emotions amplifies it and your actions increase its momentum.

KEY NUMBER ONE HUNDRED FOUR

Don't go out searching for it; stay in to prepare for it. The universe seldom brings us the things we say we want if our actions haven't shown our commitment to our words. In nature, there is a stage, time, or season of preparation before a birth or manifestation can occur. Some things require space: space to grow in healthy circumstances; space to be nourished and flourish. Other things require security: a safe state of existence; protection to mature past its defenseless infancy stage. Whatever the requirements; if we have not aligned our life to facilitate what we say we want, then it's probably not coming by way of natural and/or perfect manifestation.

CHAPTER TEN

MANIFESTING

You've been equipped and enlightened, now the world is yours and the universe is conspiring to bring good things to you. You are now able to change to course of the future with your thoughts. Perfect timing and divine alignment are opening up new realms of possibilities as you have begun to attract what will bring your dreams into reality. You are creating successful habits and utilizing your ability to do great things. Your stumbling blocks are now stepping stones. Here are some keys to maximize for potential as you manifest!

KEY NUMBER ONE HUNDRED FIVE

The Dos and Don'ts of Manifesting:

   a. DO remain positive and make positive affirmations.

   b. DO say is like it's already done.

   c. DO listen to crown chakra meditation music.

   d. DO meditate on what you want frequently. Keep it on your mind. Make it real in your brain, and it will be real in the physical world.

   e. DO be very intentional with your actions and decision-making.

   f. DO NOT spend time thinking about anything that is the opposite of what you desire.

   g. DO NOT dwell on negative thoughts.

   h. DO NOT entertain gossip, excuses, or slow-moving energies.

   i. DO NOT be afraid to distance yourself from those who don't believe in you.

KEY NUMBER ONE HUNDRED SIX

Abundance is a mindset but also a vibration. Like all vibrations, there are a number of ways to tap into it. Use these keys to manifest more abundance in your life:

a. Practice daily gratitude and appreciation.

b. Forgive others and yourself.

c. Say no to things you don't want to do.

d. Spend time with people you love.

e. Go where you are celebrated, not tolerated.

f. Clarify your intentions and spend time planning your goals.

g. Seek opportunities that may leave you in awe.

h. Ask the universe for assistance.

i. Cultivate joy throughout the day.

j. Laugh and find humor in life.

k. Shift your energy through movement.

l. Work on a passion project.

m. Meditate.

n. Invest in yourself and your education.

o. Seek out wisdom through connections with others.

p. Clear out mental and physical clutter.

q. Learn something new.

KEY NUMBER ONE HUNDRED SEVEN

When manifesting, meditation is a valuable tool. As you gain momentum and may find more demands on your time, do not break away from the resources that have gotten you this far. Meditation every morning is like are putting on armor for the day's battles. Its grounding and centering yourself against our own impatience, deficiency, resentment, and hostility.The essence of power is the ability to keep your initiative. Power is the ability to manifest a reality despite adversity. Old energy is clearing. New energy is entering. Great things are coming. Be patient and work your plan with full faith and a clear mind.

KEY NUMBER ONE HUNDRED EIGHT

Signs you are on the right path of manifesting you:

a. You find purpose despite life's burdens.

b. The right people are being attracted to you.

c. Your circumstances are getting better.

d. You feel better about yourself and future

e. You're building momentum and seeing progress and results

f. You're experiences favorable coincidences.

g. You feel more peace than anxiety.

KEY NUMBER ONE HUNDRED NINE

See the opportunity and not the opposition. Approach each task like it's your turn to make the game winning shot. Maneuveraround disappointments and difficulties as a basketball player would out wit or out work his opponents on the court. Also, don't forget to pass the ball to your teammates. You will accomplish more as a unified collective. As you are manifesting, encourage and build those around you.

KEY NUMBER ONE HUNDRED TEN

Form an alliance within yourself that states all parts of you will conduct themselves in a manner that prospers and protects the others above all else. Daily, each component will be accountable for the others. For example: Me, myself, and I all watch each other's back. My mind, soul and body have each other's best interest at heart. This 3 cord strand is cosmically unbreakable. Your mind should think in support of your soul. Your soul should pull your body for environments that are best for you. Your body should be active in efforts to further the will of your mind and soul. You are a trinity and your greatest trifecta.

KEY NUMBER ONE HUNDRED ELEVEN

Act on your intuitive thoughts without delay. Your intuition is perfect, timeless, and divine perception. Since your mind's eye does not exist in the structure of time that we identify with, often when we have a gut feeling or an instant idea, it is necessary to immediately respond accordingly, as you may be at the gateway of opportunity by way of universal alignment. Promptly carrying out the will of your intentions through corresponding actions will get you to your destination much faster than even dedication and hard work. Call that person; write down that idea; make that connection; settle that vendetta. Whatever it is; do it when the thought comes into your mind. You never know what the universe has set up for you and is waiting for you to respond to the call of your spirit.

AFTERWORD

"Morning meditation, spiritual devotion/
Anytime you get off-purpose, realign your focus/
No matter what their opinion; remember that you're
chosen."

Great day and grand risings! You are a divine being! You are no longer the same. A major shift has occurred; a change has begun, and the transformation is visible. You glow like never before. What's within you is so illuminated that it cannot be contained in your physical casing. You have grown so much and should be so very proud of yourself. Never again will you dim your light to fit in! You will now shine brighter than ever because you know who you are, and you have freed yourself to become who you were destined to be from the very beginning. Your true self is awesome! You are worthy, and you are loved. You are a magical being of love and light. Shine your light all around and share it freely with others. Don't talk much about it; just do it. Unapologetically, be a lighthouse for those who are lost in the sea of life. It will bring you so much in return, and your inner source of light will continue to grow in powerful splendor.

Hotep is an ancient Kemetic Medu Neter word which means: May divine peace be with you on the safari of life. It can also be used as a form of greeting or farewell.

Hotep.

Brian Anthony Hyppolite

ABOUT THE AUTHOR

Award-winning 21st-century Haitian-American author and recording artist Brian A. Hyppolite has influenced and inspired elevation for over a decade, while dedicating much of his life to the art of self-mastery. A father and serial entrepreneur from Tampa, Florida, he has contributed collections of songs, poems, stories, monologues, and online content, as a mouthpiece for the lives, times, and tribulations of his people and their struggles.

The 2020 release of Hyppolite's bestselling autobiography, *Gods Don't Sit on Man-Made Thrones*, sparked its own revival amongst the underdogs, black sheep, and outcasts that identify with Hyppolite's against-all-odds presence.

From his soul-baring expressions to his in-depth, informative writings, you will never experience Hyppolite on a surface level.

CONTACT US

IF YOU NEED ASSISTANCE WITH MANIFESTING YOU AND EVERYTHING YOU DESIRE IN LIFE AND YOU NEED ACCOUNTABILITY, JOIN US IG: @MANIFEST_UNIVERSITY.